LOOK !

There's a Dog at School

Annette Van Zetten

Print information available on the last page

Rev. date: 07/12/2016

To order additional copies of this book, contact:
Xlibris
1-800-455-039
www.xlibris.com.au
Orders@Xlibris.com.au

This book belongs to:

_____

_____

In memory of my mum Thurline and sister Coral. Two of my favourite people, who loved life and enjoyed a rhyme.

Written and illustrated by Annette Van Zetten

Hope you enjoy our story.

To order additional copies of this book within Australia, contact:
www.annettevanzetten.com

Summer became a Story Dog in 2011 and is proudly supported by Bambrick media.

For more information on the Story Dogs program, go to

www.storydogs.org.au

LOOK!

THERE'S A DOG AT SCHOOL

This story is about a dog named Summer,
all who meet her seem to **love** her.

She has some mates,
who she thinks are great.

First there is Henry,
a little pup.
To say hello,
he jump,
jump,
jumps!

Then there is Ninja who likes to play chase.
I think he could win any **race!**

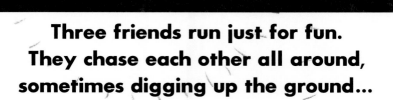

Three friends run just for fun.
They chase each other all around,
sometimes digging up the ground...

More friends of Summer are Chloe and Ella.
When Summer sits nicely Chloe will pat her.

Chloe likes to brush Summer's hair.
Bits fly away in the air.

Even though it makes a mess,
the birds could use it for their nest.

Summer gives Ella's little toes a sniff.
Do you think it tickles just a bit?

New baby Vincent is too small to play,
so Summer sits by as he sleeps all day.

Summer is so happy when friends come to play,
but she has an important job for today.

Going to school is what Summer likes best.
She wears her special orange vest.

Summer **jumps** in the car taking her seat,
excited to see the new friends she will meet.

Down the path and through the gate,

Summer the Story Dog does **not** like to be **late!**

"**Look!** There's a dog at school",
the children all say.
"Is she allowed to come and play"?

Give her a pat and say hello,
then off to work she must go.

Her important job ahead, is...

...to listen quietly,
while the books are read.

The children are waiting to give her a pat,
then all settle down and sit on the mat.

Excited to see what the story will be,
Summer listens and waits patiently.

Stories with monkeys swinging in trees,
fairies drinking pink cups of tea.

Birds with babies in a nest,
a dog on a surfboard Summer liked **best**.

Summer's school day is over,
all the books have been read.

They now say goodbye,
and give pats on her head.

The time goes so fast, now back into class.

Home for a rest,
curled up on her bed,
she remembers the stories,
and dreams fill her head.

Summer knows she is a special puppy,
not many dogs are so lucky.

She gets to see all the children at school...

It's lovely to have good friends.
Try to be a good friend like Summer.

Speak nicely and be kind to others,
especially to animals
and your sisters and brothers.

Before you pat a stranger's dog,
always,
check with the owner,
and wait until they say;

Yes, that will be OK.

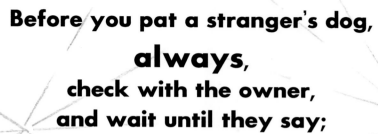

Printed in the United States
By Bookmasters